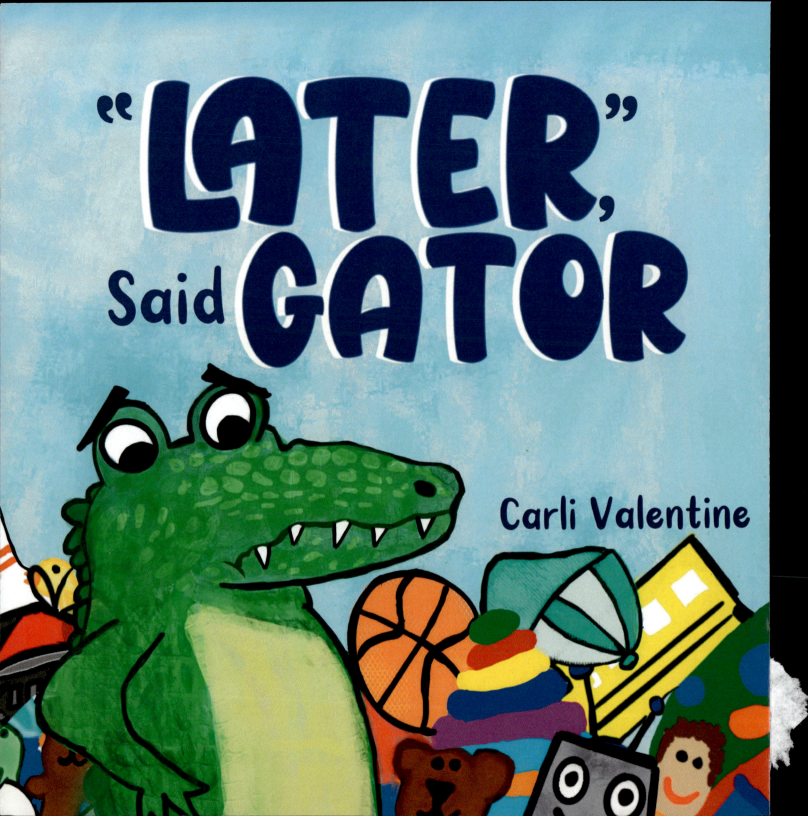

To my boys—
Always know that with hard work and determination you are capable of anything!
—C.V.

Be Mighty Like Mico!

He dislikes cleaning **messes** and says he'll do it **LATER!**

He's always planning something with his BIG **imagination**.

His **creative** "juice" is flowing, as he paints with all his **heart**.

"I'm busy right this minute.
I'll clean it all up later,"
says a **CLEVER** and **INVENTIVE**
EXTRA-FOCUSED little gator. . . .

Milo's feeling **ANXIOUS**,
with no time to clean his mess.
He's back to working on his
robot—**TOTALLY OBSESSED**!

He's busy on his project,
but begins to have the **WIGGLES**.

He finds his special basketball
and **DANCES** while he dribbles.

His mama pops her head in
and seems a bit distraught.

His room is a **DISASTER**!
It looks like he's been **CAUGHT**!

She tries to keep composure
but is feeling rather mad.
"Milo, I know you're playing,
but this mess has buried Chad."

Milo groans and rolls his eyes.
He's **SASSY** as can be!
He'll clean the mess up later.
He's **BUSY**. Can't she see?

His ball continues bouncing, knocking something to the ground. Books go flying everywhere, the mess is **ALL AROUND**!

A little while later,
he starts to **PLAY** with rocks.
INSPECTING his collection,
he leaves an empty box.

Milo looks across the room and sees his tub of blocks. Soon **FORGETTING** all about his **SPECIAL** shiny rocks.

Blocks in every color, in different shapes and sizes. Milo can build anything—he loves to make **SURPRISES**.

Milo uses every block.
He stacks them to the ceiling.

 Then he sees his **TRICYCLE**,

and **ZOOM**

he's off and **WHEELING**.

The mess is piling up now.
It's filling his whole room!

He doesn't feel prepared to clean
but says he'll do it **SOON**!

Then suddenly he sees it—his **FAVORITE** purple cup.
He dives and digs to grab it. . .

...and a giant mess ERUPTS!

He's **STUCK** beneath the pile.
He tries to look around.
The heap has **TAKEN OVER**!

WILL HE EVER BE FOUND?

He tries to dig them out.
The **MESS** is way too **BIG**!

So Mama grabs a shovel and quickly starts to dig!

He wants to **CHANGE** his ways
and clean this giant mess.
"**ALL** gators make **MISTAKES**, my dear,
and I don't **LOVE** you any less!"

They **WORK TOGETHER** quickly to put it all away.
They gather things in piles and clean without delay.

Milo finally understands
what Mama had been saying!
By cleaning things along the way,
he'll have more time for playing.

He knows it will take **PRACTICE** to become a bit more **TIDY**. Together they devise a plan to make his new skill **MIGHTY**!

His mom will set a timer that dings to let him know to take a break and **CLEAN** . . . then back to **PLAY** he'll go.

You <u>CAN</u> do it!

Milo's Mighty Cleanup Tips

Here are some tips that can make cleaning up a lot easier!

1. Use timers to encourage cleanup time between activities. Set goals for how long it will take you to do different cleaning tasks. Using a timer can make cleaning up more exciting—a "race against the clock."

2. Make a pile of everything that needs to be put away. Then, separate into similar groupings. Example: put all the books together in a pile, blocks in a pile, gather dirty clothes together, etc. By grouping big tasks into smaller ones, the cleaning process will be much more manageable.

3. Create a checklist of important goals that should be achieved in the cleaning process. Using a checklist can be highly motivating and rewarding!

4. Make cleaning fun! Example: turn on some music to dance together while you clean. After each "mini task" is achieved, take a quick break or have a little snack to celebrate. Get creative and come up with your own ways to make cleaning fun!

5. Designate a spot to put things. Make sure to have bins, baskets, or bags that can contain groupings of items. Example: label a bin for legos, one for blocks, one for superheroes, etc.

6. Work together with a parent or friend to clean. They may have suggestions that will help make things easier.

7. A reward chart can also be used to help motivate you to keep things picked up along the way.

8. Be patient with yourself! With practice and a bit of work, your NEW CLEANING SKILLS will be MIGHTY like MILO's!

About the Author
Carli Valentine

Carli Valentine is a children's book author and illustrator. She resides with her husband, Keaton and 2 boys (Finnegan and Lochlan) in Ogden, Utah. When she's not sketching or scribbling down ideas for her children's books she likes to hang out with family, volunteer at her son's elementary school, and dedicates her time to various children's heart defect charities.

More Books By Carli Valentine

Coming soon . . .
More books in this collection!

This is a work of fiction. Names, characters, places, and incidents are either the product of the author's imagination or are used fictitiously. Any resemblance to actual persons, living or dead, events, or locales is entirely coincidental.

Text and Illustration Copyright © 2023 Carli Valentine
Book design by Carli Valentine
Editing by Andrea Ketchelmeier

Published in 2023 by Design By Valentine LLC, in North Ogden, UT, USA. All rights reserved. No part of this book may be reproduced or used in any manner without written permission of the copyright owner except for the use of quotations in a book review. For more information, address: carliavalentine@gmail.com

First paperback edition January 2023

Printed and bound in the United States

Book authored and illustrated by Carli Valentine

Library of Congress Control Number:
2023901452

ISBN (Paperback)- 978-1-957505-12-1
ISBN (Hardcover)- 978-1-957505-13-8

Visit www.carlivalentine.com
www.instagram.com/carlivalentineauthor
www.facebook.com/Carli-Valentine-Childrens-Book-AuthorIllustrator-102280112241008/
www.amazon.com/Carli-Valentine/e/B09JL7V5NB/

Made in the USA
Monee, IL
03 March 2023